HISTORY IN LITERATURE

THE STORY BEHIND...

F. SCOTT FITZGERALD'S

THE GREAT GATSBY

Laura J. Hensley

Heinemann LIBRARY

www.heinemann.co.uk/library

Visit our website to find out more information about Heinemann Library books.

To order:

 Phone 44 (0) 1865 888066

 Send a fax to 44 (0) 1865 314091

 Visit the Heinemann Bookshop at www.heinemann.co.uk/library to browse our catalogue and order online.

First published in Great Britain by
Heinemann Library, Halley Court, Jordan Hill, Oxford,
OX2 8EJ, part of Harcourt
Education. Heinemann is a registered
trademark of Harcourt Education Ltd.
© Harcourt Education Ltd 2007
The moral right of the proprietor has been asserted.

Editorial: Louise Galpine, Lucy Beevor,
and Rosie Gordon
Design: Richard Parker and Manhattan Design
Maps: International Mapping
Picture Research: Melissa Allison
and Ginny Stroud-Lewis
Production: Camilla Crask
Originated by Modern Age
Printed and bound in China by Leo Paper Group Ltd

10 digit ISBN 0 431 08170 0
13 digit ISBN 978 0 431 08170 0
11 10 09 08 07
10 9 8 7 6 5 4 3 2 1

British Library Cataloguing in Publication Data
Hensley, Laura J.
  The story behind The great Gatsby. - (History in
  literature)
813.5'2
A full catalogue record for this book is available from
the British Library.

Acknowledgements
The publishers would like to thank the following for
permission to reproduce photographs/ quotes: **p.
41,** Alamy Images/DIOMEDIA; **p. 33,** Art Resource,
NY/Schomburg Center, The New York Public Library; **p.
14,** Teaching old dogs new tricks', front cover of 'Life'
magazine, 18th February, 1926 (colour litho), Held,
John (Junior) (1889-1958) Bridgeman Art Library/
New-York Historical Society, New York, USA; **pp. 16,
40,** Corbis; **pp. 4, 6, 10, 17, 26, 20, 21, 22, 28, 30, 31,
32, 35 right, 36, 38, 43, 46,** Corbis/Bettmann; **p. 42,**
Corbis/Geoffrey Clements; **p. 12,** Corbis/H. Armstrong
Roberts; **p. 27,** Corbis/John Springer Collection; **p.
8,** Corbis/Lake County Museum; **p. 39,** Corbis/North
Carolina Museum of Art; **pp. 18, 19,** Corbis/Underwood
& Underwood; **p. 5,** Getty Images/Hulton Archive; **pp.
15, 25, 34, 35 left, 44** Getty Images/Hulton Archive; **p.
48,** Getty Images/Roger Viollet; **p. 29,** Getty Images/
Time & Life Pictures; **pp. 13, 37** Image courtesy of The
Advertising Archives; **pp. 9, 45** Princeton University;
p. 49, The Kobal Collection/Paramount; **p. 47,** The
Library of Congress. Jacket cover for the first edition
of THE GREAT GATSBY by F. Scott Fitzgerald (New
York, Scribner, 1925) provided by Princeton University
library. Used by permission of Scribner, an imprint of
Simon and Schuster Adult Publishing Group. **Cover**
Corbis/Bettmann; background photos.com, istockpho-
to.com.1) David Higham Associates for quotes from
The Great Gatsby - UK and Commonwealth only
2) Reprinted with permission of Scribner, an imprint
of Simon & Schuster Adult Publishing Group, from
The Great Gatsby by F Scott Fitzgerald. © 1925 by
Charles Scribner's Sons. © renewed 1953 by Frances
Scott Fitzgerald Lanahan 3) Quotes from various texts
by F Scott Fitzgerald with permission of David Higham
Associates – UK and Commonwealth rights 4) p6;
p27; p47 - Reprinted with permission of Scribner, an
imprint of Simon & Schuster Adult Publishing Group,
from F Scott Fitzgerald: A LIFE IN LETTERS, edited
by Matthew J Bruccoli. © 1994 by the Trustees under
Agreement dated July 3 1975, created by Frances
Scott Fitzgerald Smith 5) P 5 - Quote by F Scott Fitzgerald from The Crack-up, © 1945 by New Directions
Publishing Corp, reprinted by permission 6) Reprinted
with permission of Scribner, an imprint of Simon and
Schuster Adult Publishing Group, from the Letters of
F. Scott Fitzgerald, edited by Andrew Turnbull © 1963
by Frances Scott Fitzgerald Lanahan © renewed 1991

The publisher would like to thank Matthew J.
Broccoli for his assistance in the preparation of
this book.

Contents

Some words are shown in bold, **like this**. You can find out what they mean by looking in the glossary.

King of the Jazz Age

After World War I ended in 1918, many people questioned the traditions and values that had allowed such a deadly war to happen. They were eager to reject the past and to replace it with their own new, modern culture.

In the United States, the economy boomed in the 1920s. Armed with money, a new generation created a lifestyle based on parties and spending. Young women adopted **flapper** styles, which, "shockingly", involved showing their knees and cutting their hair short. These fashions allowed a new freedom of movement, so were all the better for doing new dances, such as the charleston. New technologies brought new inventions such as radios, **phonographs**, and films. They quickly spread daring new trends, such as **jazz** music, all across the country, and launched the careers of new celebrities. Perhaps the ultimate rebellious gesture of the era was drinking alcohol, which had been made illegal in the US in 1919.

In the 1920s, young people eagerly embraced new trends and dances. Here, flappers dance the charleston.

No figure represented this period, known as the Roaring Twenties, better than the US writer F. Scott Fitzgerald. Beginning in 1920, at age 23, Fitzgerald made a splash with novels and short stories detailing the wild lives of this new generation. He even invented the term "Jazz Age" to describe the era. Beyond writing about the new culture, Fitzgerald also lived it. He and his free-spirited wife, Zelda, made headlines for their all-night parties, wild stunts, and glamorous friends. These experiences directly inspired Fitzgerald's writing.

F. Scott Fitzgerald, shown here in 1925, is now considered one of the most important US writers of all time.

In 1925, Fitzgerald published his **modernist** masterpiece, *The Great Gatsby*. Set in 1922, the novel tells of Jay Gatsby's **quest** to win back the love of the beautiful and wealthy Daisy Buchanan. In this novel, Fitzgerald used a writing style that captured the glittering side of the Jazz Age, such as the new-found wealth, parties, music, and dancing. Beneath this glitter, however, Fitzgerald exposed the dark underside of an era built on **material possessions**, including lawlessness, **elitism**, and a lack of deeper values. Fitzgerald's novel suggested that such a **superficial** culture was headed towards disaster. Indeed, the **stock market crash** of 1929 brought everything to a screeching halt. Because of its insight into both the surface and the soul of this period, *The Great Gatsby* is seen as an important record of the era, as well as one of American literature's greatest novels.

In 1937, Fitzgerald wrote (about the Roaring Twenties):

> *America was going on the greatest, gaudiest spree in history and there was going to be plenty to tell about it. … All the stories that came into my head had a touch of disaster in them – the lovely creatures in my novels went to ruin … my millionaires were … beautiful and damned.*

Early Life

Francis Scott Key Fitzgerald was born on 24 September, 1896 in St. Paul, Minnesota. Scott, as he was known, was named after Francis Scott Key, a cousin who wrote the "Star Spangled Banner", the US national anthem.

Childhood

Scott's father, Edward, had the manners and sophistication of the upper class, but was in fact a failed businessman who struggled to support his family. Scott's mother, Mollie McQuillan, was a plain, modest woman. She came from a family of Irish **immigrants** that had recently become wealthy through the grocery business. From 1898 to 1908, the Fitzgeralds lived in Buffalo and Syracuse, New York, where Edward worked as a salesman. In 1901, Scott's sister, Annabel, was born.

When Edward lost his job in 1908, the family moved back to St. Paul. From this point on, Scott's family lived largely on money from his mother's family. Although they could barely afford it, they lived in the fashionable Summit Avenue area of the city, and sent Scott to the best schools. However, Scott felt like an outsider because of his lack of money, compared to his wealthy classmates, and because of his status as a Catholic among Protestants.

As a boy, F. Scott Fitzgerald discovered he had a talent for writing.

In 1938, Fitzgerald wrote in a letter:

That was always my experience – a poor boy in a rich town; a poor boy in a rich boy's school ... However, I have never been able to forgive the rich for being rich, and it has coloured my entire life and works.

School years

At the private St. Paul Academy, Scott longed to be popular. He tried to get on to sports teams, despite his small size, and worked to establish himself as a leader. He did not always achieve social success, but he found he had a gift for writing.

Because of his low marks, Scott's parents decided he needed the discipline of boarding school. In 1911, he left for Hackensack, New Jersey, where he attended the Catholic Newman School. In time, he again found his place by writing poems, plays, and stories.

This map shows St. Paul, Minnesota and Syracuse and Buffalo, New York, where Fitzgerald lived as a boy and young man.

CATHOLICISM IN THE USA

In **colonial** America, the vast majority of settlers were Protestant, while less than one per cent of the population was Catholic. By the mid-1800s, however, more Catholic immigrants began to come to the United States.

In the 1850s, a political party called the American Party (nicknamed the "Know-Nothing Party") rose to power because of its anti-Catholic and anti-immigrant beliefs. The party's American-born Protestant members feared that Catholic immigrants would take their jobs or, worse, gain political power and then force Catholicism on the country. The party's ideas included restricting **immigration**, particularly from Catholic countries such as Ireland, and keeping immigrants and Catholics out of politics. In 1855, there were nearly 45 members of this party in government. By 1860, however, the party had distntegrated because members had differing views on slavery.

In the 1890s, when Fitzgerald was born, the American Protective Association gained power based on similar anti-Catholic aims. Members wanted to prevent Catholic people, foreign-born or not, from having a job where they might influence others. At its peak, the group had over two million members.

Princeton

As school came to an end, Fitzgerald decided that Princeton University, in Princeton, New Jersey, was the only college for him. He was drawn to the glamour of the East coast, as he would be for the rest of his life – and as the midwestern characters in *The Great Gatsby* would be.

In the autumn of 1913, Fitzgerald started at Princeton and once again focused on becoming a popular figure. Some classmates, however, thought he tried too hard to be the centre of attention. Once again, he felt poor compared to his peers, who came from the wealthiest families and the most **elite** schools in the country. Also, as a Catholic, he was again in the minority.

Fitzgerald remained proud of his Princeton connection for the rest of his life.

A developing talent

Fitzgerald never became a leader, but he made a name for himself through his writing. He wrote lyrics for musical comedies, produced by the university's "Triangle Club", and had poems and stories published in the university's literary magazine. He also became friends with John Peale Bishop and Edmund Wilson, two men who would one day become important literary **critics**. At one point, Fitzgerald declared to Wilson, "I want to be one of the greatest writers who ever lived, don't you?" He did not focus on his studies, however, failing many courses and eventually falling a year behind his contemporaries.

In 1917, as the United States entered World War I (see page 11), Fitzgerald joined the army. By the autumn of his final year, he reported for training. He would never graduate from university.

Ginevra King

Daisy (Fay) Buchanan, the "dream girl" at the centre of The Great Gatsby, *was in many ways inspired by a young woman named Ginevra King (above). Fitzgerald went out with Ginevra while he was a student at Princeton.*

Fitzgerald met Ginevra, a beautiful, wealthy 16-year-old from Chicago, in January 1915, while at home in St. Paul for the winter holidays. The pair soon fell in love and began a long-distance romance that was filled with passionate letters. In time, however, Ginevra's family made it clear to Fitzgerald that, as he wrote in his journals, "Poor boys shouldn't think of marrying rich girls".

Ginevra officially broke things off in January 1917. By the autumn of 1918 she had become engaged to a young man who, like Daisy's husband, Tom, came from a very wealthy Chicago family. Ginevra also had a good friend named Edith Cummings who was a champion golfer, like the Jordan Baker character in The Great Gatsby *(see page 29). Following his relationship with Ginevra, Fitzgerald's feelings of social and romantic rejection would inspire his greatest works, including* The Great Gatsby.

Meeting Zelda

In June 1918, Fitzgerald was sent to Camp Sheridan, near Montgomery, Alabama. However, he was often more interested in socializing and meeting girls than in training for war. At a country club dance in July 1918, he met Zelda Sayre, the daughter of an Alabama Supreme Court judge. Scott and Zelda danced together and flirted, but, like Daisy in *The Great Gatsby*, Zelda had a long string of **suitors**.

Zelda was wild and individual. She loved pranks, such as calling the fire brigade to say someone was on the roof – before climbing up there herself.

She also stayed out all night, which was shocking for a young woman of the time. Once Scott managed to gain Zelda's attention, the two of them quickly found that they had the same approach to life. They both loved fun and parties, and both dreamed of becoming glamorous, famous figures. Zelda's parents did not approve of the relatively poor young man courting their daughter. Scott and Zelda nonetheless began a passionate romance.

Scott and Zelda's relationship was fiery and passionate from the start.

Early struggles

World War I ended before Fitzgerald could be sent to fight. In early 1919, he moved to New York. There, he hoped to earn enough money to marry Zelda and provide her with a comfortable lifestyle. He worked as a writer in advertising, and in his spare time he tried to sell short stories to magazines. He struggled to earn money and, in June 1919, Zelda broke off their engagement.

Fitzgerald moved back to his parents' home in St. Paul. He wanted to focus all of his energy on becoming a successful writer and winning Zelda back. In September 1919, his novel *This Side of Paradise* was accepted for publication. In the winter of 1920, Zelda began seeing him again, and the couple married that spring.

At the beginning of World War I, much of Europe was divided between the Allied Powers and the Central Powers.

"THE WAR TO END ALL WARS"

*Since 1867, several countries throughout a large section of Europe were united within the Austro-Hungarian Empire (see the map, above). On 28 June, 1914, Archduke Franz Ferdinand, **heir** to the Austro-Hungarian throne, visited Sarajevo in Bosnia. During this visit, Ferdinand was assassinated by Gavrilo Princep, a 19-year-old Bosnian **Serb** who resented Austro-Hungarian rule over **Slavs** and Serbs. Austria-Hungary blamed Serbia for the assassination and eventually declared war on this neighbouring country. This resulted in a series of **alliances**: the Central Powers, mainly Austria-Hungary, Germany, and Turkey, were on one side, and the Allies, mainly France, Great Britain, Russia, Italy, Japan, and Serbia, were on the other.*

*At first, the United States, under President Woodrow Wilson, remained **neutral**. But in early 1917, Germany attacked US merchant ships, killing several Americans. On 6 April, 1917, the United States entered the war on the side of the Allies. The US presence gave tired Allied troops the boost they needed, and by the autumn of 1918 the Central Powers were defeated. By the end of World War I, about 8.5 million soldiers had died, a loss that devastated Western society.*

The Jazz Age

When Fitzgerald's book, *This Side of Paradise*, was published on 26 March, 1920, it was an instant bestseller. Highly **autobiographical**, it told of university life and the wild habits of a new generation. Fitzgerald was only 23 at the time, and the handsome young author quickly became a celebrity, along with his wife, Zelda.

A new world power

The Fitzgeralds' newfound celebrity happened at an important moment in US history. The economies of Europe were damaged by the devastation of World War I, but the United States had entered the War late and had seen no fighting on its own land. It emerged with relatively little damage.

At the same time, the post war period in the United States saw a rise in new products, such as cars and household appliances. This created new jobs that paid well, which in turn made ordinary people willing to spend more. Increasingly, people spent their extra money on leisure activities and material possessions.

Women had more freedom and independence in the 1920s than ever before.

Edna St. Vincent Millay (1892–1950)

"My candle burns at both ends
It will not last the night
But ah, my foes, and oh, my friends –
It gives a lovely light!"

Born in 1892, US poet Edna St. Vincent Millay was seen as a voice for the "new women" of the 1920s. She lived what many saw as a shocking lifestyle – drinking and smoking with men, and carrying on passionate love affairs. Her poems captured the youthful spirit of the era. In this famous passage, the candle burning at both ends symbolizes pushing

A new generation

Young people began to question their parents' conservative, **Victorian** values and traditions, which **conformed** to what society considered normal. The new generation felt that these old-fashioned values had failed to prevent the War, which then claimed the lives of so many. In the United States, young people, such as the Fitzgeralds, were eager to create a new world for themselves.

During the War, many US women had filled some of the jobs left empty by men who had gone to fight, such as jobs in transport or in factories. This gave them a taste of independence that they were not willing to give up. Also, in 1920, a law called the 19th Amendment was passed, which gave women the right to vote. Unlike the previous generation, which had preferred quiet women who stayed at home, this new generation allowed women to be seen and heard as never before.

This advertisement for Bally shoes shows the typical hairstyle, fashion, and make-up adopted by flappers in the 1920s.

FLAPPERS

*To reflect their independence, young women such as Zelda embraced new fashions. Their mothers had worn tight, restricting **corsets** and kept their skin covered, but this new generation of women wore loose-fitting, drop-waisted dresses that allowed movement and freedom. They also dared to show their knees. Dresses were often made of rayon, a new synthetic fabric that was cheap and washable. In contrast to the pinned-up, long hair of their mothers, which was seen as a symbol of femininity, Zelda and others cut their hair into short **bobs**. These short hairstyles were complemented by cloche hats, which were close fitting and rounded, just barely leaving room for a woman's bob to show at the bottom. Women began to experiment with make-up, something that had been used mostly by actresses and prostitutes during the Victorian era. They also drank alcohol and smoked cigarettes in public. These women became known as flappers, and they represented all that was modern and new.*

FEBRUARY 18, 1926 Teaching old Dogs new tricks PRICE 15 CENTS

"Flaming youth"

As the 1920s progressed, it became clear that members of the so-called "flaming youth"– flappers and the young men back from war – were forming a rebellious new **youth culture**. This period in history has been called the Roaring Twenties or, by Fitzgerald himself, the Jazz Age.

The artwork of John Held Jr. captured the lively rhythms of the Jazz Age, as shown on this cover of *Life* magazine from 18 February, 1926.

The birth of jazz

Parties were at the centre of the new youth culture, and at the centre of the Fitzgeralds' lifestyle. These parties were often driven by the lively beat of a new form of music, known as jazz.

Jazz originated among African Americans, who blended traditions from West Africa with elements of **blues** and **ragtime**. First popular in New Orleans, jazz moved to Chicago, and then to New York. The music had an energetic sound with complex rhythms. Musicians would often perform **improvised** solos instead of following the notes on the page exactly. It has been said that jazz was the first truly American art form. Famous jazz musicians of the 1920s included Louis Armstrong, Fats Waller, Jelly Roll Morton, Fletcher Henderson, and Duke Ellington.

New dances

Young fans of jazz developed lively new dance styles to accompany the music. Dances such as the charleston and one step matched the jazz rhythms. The previous generation had limited itself to formal ballroom dances with strict rules and rigid posture, but the new dances allowed for personal expression and wild, enthusiastic kicks and arm gestures.

Louis Armstong (centre, back) performs with "King" Oliver's Creole Jazz Band in 1923.

Louis Armstrong (1901–1971)

Louis Armstrong was born in 1901 in New Orleans, the birthplace of jazz. From an early age, he gained a reputation as a talented musician in local bands. After moving to New York and Chicago in the 1920s, his extraordinary ability as a trumpet player and his lively, charming personality quickly made him a star. He became a popular soloist in bands such as the Hot Seven. The public came to know him by the nickname Satchmo, which was short for Satchelmouth (a satchel is a large bag), because he seemed able to get "bags" of air into his cheeks.

Over the course of his long career, Armstrong introduced a new, catchy kind of jazz known as swing. He also developed a style of singing without words, known as scat. He became a world-renowned star of radio, films, and international concert tours. He is remembered as one of the greatest jazz musicians of all time.

Speakeasies

Jazz Age parties were not only fuelled by music and dancing – alcohol often played a central role. This, too, was a show of rebellion, because in 1919 the 18th Amendment, a law known as **Prohibition**, made alcohol illegal in the United States. Many people lost respect for laws that seemed out of touch with modern living, and they broke the law by buying illegal alcohol. (Unfortunately, for the Fitzgeralds, and many others, too much drinking would eventually lead to serious personal and health problems.) Many Americans also went to bars known as speakeasies, where alcohol was served. Speakeasies were generally run by **organized crime**, which was the era's most violent example of breaking the rules (see pages 30–31).

The rise of celebrities

In the 1920s, young people developed an interest in knowing about the high-profile celebrities who represented their generation. This interest was fed in 1919, when the *Illustrated Daily News* (later *New York Daily News*) was introduced. This started the trend of **tabloid** newspapers, that focused on scandals, celebrities, and gossip. Suddenly, people began to follow and admire celebrities in the way our society does today.

Film stars

Cinema became extremely popular in the 1920s, with ticket sales doubling over the course of the decade. Films of this era were silent until 1927, when *The Jazz Singer* became the first "talkie". It featured an orchestral soundtrack, some recorded dialogue, and singing by the singer Al Jolson.

The elegant and handsome Rudolph Valentino, shown here with Vilma Banky in *The Son of the Sheik* (1926), had an enormous number of fans.

Along with the popularity of films came the rise of the film star. Tabloids featured a constant flow of gossip about movie actors, while mass-circulation magazines specifically about films provided fans with gossip and information on how to copy stars' hairstyles and fashions. Actors such as Charlie Chaplin, Buster Keaton, Rudolph Valentino, Mary Pickford, Clara Bow, and Douglas Fairbanks became household names with loyal fans. When Valentino died suddenly in 1926, at age 31, an estimated 100,000 mourners attended his funeral in New York.

Recording stars

Musicians also became popular celebrities, thanks, in part, to new technologies. Over the course of the 1920s, the phonograph became popular, and it allowed young people to buy recordings and listen to them in their homes. At the same time, radio became increasingly important. The first public broadcast in the United States was made in 1920, in Pittsburgh, and by the mid-1920s many US homes had a radio. Performers such as Louis Armstrong (see page 15) and Paul Whiteman, who previously would have had fans only in their particular regions, found that they were now national, and sometimes international, stars.

Charles Lindbergh (1902–1974)

*Charles Lindbergh was one of the best-loved celebrities of the 1920s. Born in 1902 and raised in Minnesota, Lindbergh developed an interest in **aviation** as a young man. He worked as an airmail pilot and a stunt flyer. In the mid-1920s, he began to think about how he could cross the Atlantic non-stop as a solo pilot. With the financial help of some St. Louis businessmen, Lindbergh helped design a single-engine plane that could make the flight. On 20–21 May, 1927, he flew this plane, Spirit of St. Louis, from New York to Paris in 33½ hours. Tabloid newspapers, magazines, and radio programs reported on every detail, and he instantly became a US and international hero, representing the new, modern generation.*

In 1932, this intense public interest in Lindbergh took a tragic turn, when the nation became fascinated by the kidnapping of his 20-month-old son, Charles Jr. The public followed the story very closely, reading about the family's negotiations with the kidnappers. Sadly, the boy was found dead ten weeks after he had been taken from his family home in New Jersey. The Lindberghs were never able to mourn their loss in private, as public interest continued through the trial and execution of the alleged kidnapper in 1936. In 1935, in desperate need of privacy, the Lindberghs moved to Europe, where public interest in them was less intense.

Charles Lindbergh stands in front of the *Spirit of St. Louis*, 20 May, 1927.

The king and queen of the Jazz Age

No couple better **embodied** this new Jazz Age culture than Scott and Zelda Fitzgerald. Tabloid newspapers eagerly reported on the beautiful couple's lives, which included wild parties, riding on the tops of taxis, and jumping fully clothed into the fountain in front of New York's Plaza Hotel.

Fitzgerald's eye for the details of his own lifestyle – the music, dances, fashions, slang, and conversation topics – gave his writing a ring of truth, making him seem like a spokesperson for a new generation. Zelda's fashionable appearance, love of adventure, and "flaming self respect", as Fitzgerald described it, made her his perfect flapper **heroine**. Throughout Fitzgerald's career, Zelda would be the inspiration for many of his female characters.

Fitzgerald followed *This Side of Paradise* with a series of short stories, published both in magazines and as collections in book form. These stories, with titles such as "Bernice Bobs Her Hair" (1920) and "The Diamond as Big as the Ritz" (1922), described the developing youth movement.

CRAZY STUNTS

Scott and Zelda were not alone in performing wild stunts. In fact, a trend for this kind of behaviour developed during the 1920s. Young people would try crazy things, such as sitting on top of a flagpole for as long as possible, or even dancing the charleston on the wing of an airplane (or on a high ledge, as above). Such stunts were perhaps a way to release the built-up tension and sadness caused by World War I. By openly celebrating silliness and fun, this generation hoped to establish a happier mood for the new era.

18

In a *Metropolitan* magazine interview in November 1923, Fitzgerald said:

I had no idea of originating an American flapper when I first began to write. I simply took girls whom I knew very well and, because they interested me as unique human beings, I used them for my heroines.

The Beautiful and Damned

Scott and Zelda were beginning to live too **fast**, however. All their drinking was wearing them out, and they quickly went through the money Fitzgerald made from writing on their **lavish** lifestyle of elegant rented houses, cars, fashionable clothes, and frequent parties. Also, the couple now had a baby to consider. In 1921 their only child, a daughter named Scottie, was born.

The strain that their busy, expensive lifestyle put on Scott and Zelda's relationship was expressed in Fitzgerald's next novel, *The Beautiful and Damned*. Set at the beginning of the Jazz Age, it described a glamorous couple's troubled relationship. The book sold well, but the response from literary critics was mixed.

Scott and Zelda Fitzgerald came to represent the glamour and youth of the Jazz Age.

Creating a classic

Despite all the attention he was receiving from the press, by 1922 Fitzgerald realized that he was losing focus on his life's ambition to be one of the greatest writers of all time. His drinking and late-night socializing left little time to concentrate on writing.

SHORT STORIES

The magazines of the time, especially The Saturday Evening Post, paid Fitzgerald well for his short stories. However, the magazines that paid him the most did not encourage daring, inventive writing, and so he sometimes did not feel proud of the stories that were published. Ever since he was a child, Fitzgerald cared deeply about winning approval from the people around him. In the early 1920s, however, critics were starting to write him off as someone who documented the youth culture well, but who lacked seriousness.

As the 1920s began, Fitzgerald had to focus on supporting his young family. This often meant writing short stories.

Greater ambitions

Fitzgerald wanted to focus again on a work that would establish him as a great, serious writer. He told his **editor**, Max Perkins, that this would be "something new – something extraordinary and beautiful and simple and **intricately** patterned." This work would become *The Great Gatsby*.

From 1922 to 1924, Fitzgerald lived in an expensive rented house on Great Neck, Long Island, outside New York City. Here, he intended to focus on his novel, but he was often distracted by rehearsals for a play he wrote, called *The Vegetable*, by short story writing, and by parties.

Scott, Zelda, and Scottie lived in various places in Europe from April 1924. At last, Fitzgerald found the peace and quiet he needed to focus on and finish his novel, which he now intended to be about the Jazz Age. He wrote to Perkins, "I feel I have an enormous power in me now, more than I've ever had in a way."

Also, being away from the United States gave Fitzgerald a chance to stand back and look at the wild lifestyle he had been living for the past few years. Finally, on 10 April, 1925, *The Great Gatsby* was published.

Fitzgerald struggled to find the peace and quiet he needed to write *The Great Gatsby*.

FINDING THE RIGHT TITLE

Throughout the writing process, Fitzgerald considered many titles for his book, including:

Among the Ash-Heaps and Millionaires
Gatsby
Gold-Hatted Gatsby
The High-Bouncing Lover
On the Road to West Egg
Trimalchio
Trimalchio in West Egg
Under the Red, White, and Blue

Trimalchio is a character in the Roman author Petronius' work, The Satyricon, which was written around AD 60. Like Gatsby, Trimalchio makes a show of his new money by throwing lavish parties. Fitzgerald was advised not to use a title featuring Trimalchio because most readers would not know this story or understand the connection.

A tale of the Jazz Age

The Great Gatsby tells the story of James Gatz, who was born to a poor family in North Dakota. At the age of 17, he met a wealthy, self-made man named Dan Cody. Inspired by Cody's example, James decided that he wanted a better, more glamorous life, and so he reinvented himself as Jay Gatsby.

While training for World War I, Gatsby was stationed in Louisville, Kentucky, where he met and fell in love with a beautiful, wealthy young woman named Daisy Fay. When Gatsby was shipped overseas to fight, Daisy did not wait for him. She instead chose to marry Tom Buchanan, who came from a wealthy Chicago family.

All of this is told throughout the novel in **flashback**, and the novel actually begins in 1922, five years after Gatsby's romance with Daisy. The **narrator**, Nick Carraway, has moved from America's Midwest to the East coast, settling in a small house in West Egg, outside New York City. His neighbour is the mysterious Gatsby. Guests arrive at Gatsby's mansion every night to attend parties filled with alcohol, music, and dancing. Gatsby has an enormous fortune, and many of his guests are suspicious about how he has earned this money.

Arnold Rothstein (1882–1928)

*The character of Meyer Wolfshiem is based on Arnold Rothstein (left), a real-life gambler and **bootlegger**. Rothstein had connections to the most powerful (but **corrupt**) political figures of the time, as well as to the most powerful gangsters. He used his connections to stop police from cracking down on illegal businesses such as speakeasies.*

*Rothstein is thought to be responsible for **rigging** the 1919 World Series, just as Wolfshiem is in The Great Gatsby. That year, the Chicago White Sox lost to the Cincinnati Reds. It was later revealed that eight Chicago players had been bribed to lose the series, which allowed gamblers to win on big bets against them. In 1928 Rothstein died after being shot during a poker game.*

Nick visits his cousin, Daisy (Fay) Buchanan, in the more exclusive East Egg. He becomes aware that Daisy and her husband, Tom, have a cold relationship. Tom is having an affair with Myrtle Wilson, a local woman from a lower class whose husband, George, owns a petrol station.

Nick learns that Gatsby chose his house in order to live directly across the bay from Daisy, and that he throws his lavish parties in the hope of seeing her. Once Gatsby discovers Nick's connection with Daisy, he asks Nick to arrange a meeting with her. Gatsby and Daisy then renew their love.

AN ART DECO COVER

The artist Francis Cugat created the original cover for *The Great Gatsby*. The cover shows a female face looming in the sky. The **abstract** face features eyes, a single tear, and lips. A carnival takes place in the foreground.

Fitzgerald was known as a fashionable writer, and so it made sense that Scribner's, his publisher, would choose an Art Deco cover. In the 1920s and 1930s, Art Deco was the most fashionable style of the day. Generally speaking, it was highly **stylized** and focused on **symmetry**, abstract shapes such as sunbursts, and a general air of glamour.

Art Deco could be seen in everything from architecture, to decorative objects for the home, to paintings and illustrations, such as this cover.

Fitzgerald loved Cugat's cover artwork so much that, when his novel was delayed, he pleaded with his publisher not to give it to other authors before he could use it.

A doomed dream

As Gatsby and Daisy's relationship blossoms, he feels assured that the wealth and status he has achieved are enough to win Daisy back. During a hot day the main characters spend together in New York City, Gatsby asks Daisy to leave Tom. Yet when Daisy sees the danger of leaving her safe, upper-class world, she cannot commit to Gatsby. The scene in New York ends suddenly, with Daisy driving back to East Egg with Gatsby.

As they pass Wilson's petrol station, Myrtle leaps out toward Gatsby's car, thinking Tom is behind the wheel because he had driven the car to New York earlier. Daisy drives into Myrtle, killing her, and then flees the scene. When George Wilson confronts Tom about the killing, Tom wrongly implies that Gatsby was responsible. Tom knows that Wilson is likely to go after Gatsby, and he does. Wilson goes to Gatsby's house and shoots him dead.

In the end, in contrast to the crowds that eagerly took advantage of Gatsby's parties, only one of his former guests (Owl Eyes) attends his funeral. Tom and Daisy go out town to avoid responsibility for the killings. Nick is left **disillusioned** by the carelessness of the Buchanans and by the tragedy of Gatsby's failed dream.

THE CHANGING *GATSBY*

The Great Gatsby is often described as the **definitive** novel of the Jazz Age. However, when Fitzgerald was originally planning it in the spring of 1922, he intended to set the novel in 1885.

Also, Fitzgerald originally wrote many pages about Gatsby's boyhood, but eventually decided this moved the story's focus too far from the central action in 1922. He reworked these pages into a short story called "Absolution" (which means "being forgiven"), published in 1924. Although the character names and some details are different, "Absolution" is believed to describe what Fitzgerald thought of as Gatsby's early history.

INSPIRATIONS FOR GATSBY

While living in Great Neck, New York, Fitzgerald began to think about and write The Great Gatsby. *Edward M. Fuller, another resident in Great Neck, perhaps offered inspiration for the Gatsby character. Like Gatsby, he had suddenly made a fortune and bought a huge estate. He worked in the stock market, but, as the government investigated him in a widely reported trial, it became clear that he had connections to organized crime, particularly to the gangster Arnold Rothstein (see page 22).*

Joseph Conrad (1857–1924)

One of the most notable devices used in the writing of The Great Gatsby *is the use of Nick as a narrator. In his previous work, Fitzgerald had not used a narrator who was directly involved in the action. In* The Great Gatsby, *however, he used Nick, a character who is both involved in the action and able to "talk to" the reader. This device makes the reader feel more involved in the story.*

Fitzgerald was perhaps inspired to use this device because of the work of the English author Joseph Conrad (above). In his letters, Fitzgerald commented on his admiration for Conrad's writing. Born in 1857, Conrad is best known for his book Heart of Darkness *(1902) and novels such as* Lord Jim *(1900), which deal with characters facing a harsh world. Significantly for* The Great Gatsby, *in these and other works, Conrad mastered the use of a narrator who is part of the plot.*

When Fitzgerald finished writing *The Great Gatsby*, he knew it was a great achievement. He was surprised to find that its reviews were mixed:

With [The Great Gatsby] Mr. Fitzgerald definitely deserts his earlier fiction which brought him a lot of money and a certain amount of [fame], and enters into the group of American writers who are producing the best serious fiction.

– H. B., *New York Post*

Critical reactions

Some reviewers saw *The Great Gatsby* as an important social document. One reviewer noted that it was "more contemporary [up-to-date] than any newspaper". Another said it was "American to the core, modern to the hour . . . in other words, Fitzgerald knows his times and his people".

Many reviewers also recognized that Fitzgerald had taken great steps forward in terms of style and form. His previous novel, *The Beautiful and Damned*, was widely considered to be too long and lacking in structure. In contrast, many critics appreciated how much meaning he had packed into *The Great Gatsby*, which is relatively short, and they recognized how his use of Nick as the narrator tied the story together. As one critic said, "It is beautifully and delicately balanced . . . There is not one accidental phrase in it, nor yet one obvious or blatant line." Critics also recognized Fitzgerald's beautiful writing style.

Critics who liked *The Great Gatsby* often said that it captures the wild, carefree spirit of the era.

The novel has no plot to mention . . . The book is . . . loud, . . . ugly, pointless. There seems to be no reason for its existence.

—Harvey Eagleton, *Dallas Morning News*

Early criticism

Other critics felt the central love story between Gatsby and Daisy was too **sentimental**, or even uninteresting. One critic even entitled her review "F. Scott Fitzgerald's Latest a Dud". Such critics saw the book as being superficial and overly focused on the surface appearances of the Jazz Age, just as many of his short stories had been. One critic wrote, "Find me one chemical trace of magic, life, irony, romance or mysticism in all of *The Great Gatsby* and I will bind myself to read one Scott Fitzgerald book a week for the rest of my life." Many of these critics predicted that the novel would quickly be forgotten.

First adaptations

Fitzgerald was disappointed to find that *The Great Gatsby* did not sell particularly well, especially by comparison with his first two novels. However, he was pleased when Hollywood bought the rights to it and made a silent film in 1926, and when Broadway made it into a play that same year.

Still, almost no one seemed to grasp the deeper meaning in the story. This understanding of the novel would not come until years later.

The 1926 silent film version of *The Great Gatsby* featured Lois Wilson as Dasiy Buchanan and Warner Baxter as Jay Gatsby.

In a letter of May 1925, Fitzgerald wrote:

Of all the reviews, even the most enthusiastic, not one had the slightest idea what [The Great Gatsby] was about.

Examining an era

As with Fitzgerald's previous work, *The Great Gatsby* was full of the glittering details of the Jazz Age. In fact, many see the novel as a definitive record of the glamorous side of the era – the side Scott and Zelda had lived to the fullest from 1920 to 1924.

New fortunes

At the centre of the novel is Gatsby, whose showy lifestyle embodies the incredible **prosperity** of the era. Gatsby's cars, mansion, boats, plane, and clothes all represent the major status symbols of the period.

LINCOLN

FAULTLESS precision gives that matchless reliability which makes the Lincoln car master of every travel demand – with incomparable smoothness and high speed, indefinitely sustained.

Lincoln appearance is conservative yet commanding – every detail of appointment conforming to the edicts of good taste.

Best of all – the Lincoln you drive today is the car of your pride next year and far into the future!

LINCOLN MOTOR COMPANY
Division of
Ford Motor Company

Advertisements such as this 1926 ad for the Ford Lincoln, connected cars with status.

CARS

In 1903, when Henry Ford started the Ford Motor Company, cars were only owned by the very wealthy. When Ford developed the automated **assembly line** in 1913, he could produce more cars more quickly, which allowed him to lower prices. In 1919, there were under seven million cars owned in the United States, or one for every sixteen people. By 1929, however, there would be 27 million, or nearly one for every five people.

In the novel, cars represent the social status of their owners. Given their weight, size, and speed, cars also represent an enormous amount of power. In an important scene, Nick accuses Jordan of driving dangerously, saying, "Either you ought to be more careful, or you oughtn't to drive at all." Jordan responds to this by saying that she expects other people to be careful, only she is allowed to be careless. While driving Gatsby's car, Daisy hits Myrtle and kills her. Daisy, too, refuses to take responsibility for her actions. Through the symbol of cars, the novel seems to suggest that this self-centred, careless generation of Americans is not responsible enough to deal with the power that comes with their wealthy, glamorous lifestyles.

The character of Jordan Baker was based on a real-life female golfer named Edith Cummings (shown here on the cover of *Time* magazine), who was friends with Fitzgerald's former girlfriend Ginevra King (see page 9).

FIFTEEN CENTS

VOL. IV   NO. 8   "There is but a single thundercloud——"   AUGUST 25, 1924
(See Page 28)

TIME

The Weekly News-Magazine

EDITH CUMMINGS

Modern women

The Great Gatsby is also full of glamorous, modern women. Most of the young women at Gatsby's parties are flappers. The text says that they wear the latest fashions, with their "hair shorn in strange new ways". They dance (alone or with partners), drink alcohol, and openly flirt with men.

Jordan Baker represents a new kind of confident, sporty American glamour. She is a professional golfer, something that would not previously have been dreamed of for a woman. Her independence and sportiness is reflected in the way she carries herself. As Nick remarks, "I noticed that she wore her evening-dress, all her dresses, like sports clothes." Jordan always seems bored, often yawning and appearing distracted, as if she has already been everywhere and seen everything.

Lavish parties

More so than in any other part of the book, Gatsby's parties capture the glamour and energy of the Jazz Age. Nick describes the wildness of these parties, when he says the guests "conducted themselves according to the rules associated with amusement parks". In addition to drinking and dancing, people plunge into fountains, crash their cars, and get into fiery arguments. Gatsby's varied guest lists – of people from many walks of life, including the newly powerful film business – reflect the exciting social mix of the era.

Corruption

Fitzgerald had a gift for capturing the glamorous details of the Jazz Age, but he also encouraged readers to think more deeply about the period. Beneath the glitter of *The Great Gatsby*, he revealed the dark side of this **decadent** era. In particular, he exposed how corrupt the period was.

A corrupt cast of characters

Throughout the book, Nick's traditional moral values are made clear. At one point he says, "I am one of the few honest people I have ever known". As the narrator, he is able to make his real thoughts known, and to make moral judgments.

In the end, Nick condemns almost all of the characters in the novel. He describes Jordan as "incurably dishonest" and Daisy and Tom as "careless" and "cruel". As a group, they are written off as "a rotten crowd".

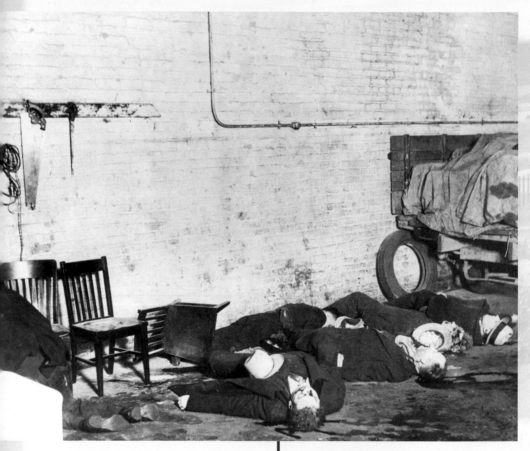

This murder became known as the St Valentine's Day Massacre (see page 31). Organized crime was the era's most obvious example of corruption.

Crime

Nick's thoughts about Gatsby are more complicated. He admires some aspects of Gatsby's character. Yet Gatsby's lifestyle is paid for by organized crime.

Gangsters saw Prohibition as an opportunity to make money, and so they started bootlegging. After tasting success, organized crime branched out and made deals with corrupt politicians. As a result, the newspaper headlines of the 1920s were often about murders and political scandals.

In the novel, it is implied that Gatsby and Wolfshiem are bootleggers, selling illegal alcohol at drugstores. They also gamble and sell stolen **bonds**. Gatsby's wealth fuels his Jazz Age lifestyle, but it is rooted in shady deals and violent associates.

Al Capone (1899–1947)

Born in 1899 to Italian immigrants, Al Capone (right) grew up in New York City. He dropped out of school as a teenager and became involved with local gangs. As a young man, his temper led him into a bar fight in which his face was slashed. From that point on, his nickname was Scarface.

In 1919 Capone's crime boss, Johnny Torrio, moved him to Chicago. After Torrio retired in 1925, Capone took over his crime network. Politicians and police officers in Chicago were often willing to take bribes, and so Capone was able to become powerful during Prohibition, when bootlegging was very popular and profitable. His criminal activities also included gambling rings and prostitution. Capone gained control of these illegal activities by having his gang murder anyone who tried to compete. Most famously, on 14 February, 1929, Capone's men murdered seven rival Irish gang members in a garage – an event now known as the St. Valentine's Day Massacre.

For years, Capone managed to avoid being charged with any crime. However, in 1931 the government managed to convict him of tax evasion (not paying his taxes). He was sent to prison, and his network eventually lost its power.

Race relations

It has sometimes been noted that nearly every character in *The Great Gatsby* is a white **Anglo-Saxon** Protestant (WASP). In some ways, this is a true reflection of the divisions of the time. In the novel, Tom Buchanan recommends a book called *The Rise of the Colored Empires* by Goddard. Tom supports the book, saying, "It's up to us [WASPs], who are the dominant race, to watch out or those other races will have control of things." Fitzgerald based Tom's ideas in this scene on a real book by Lothrop Stoddard called *The Rising Tide of Color Against White World* **Supremacy** (1920), a racist book aimed at a white readership.

Immigration

One source of fear for people like Tom was the rising level of immigration. In the late 19th and early 20th century, immigration was at a peak in the United States. After World War I, however, many Americans developed a distrust of foreigners, whom they held responsible for the War. Many also feared, just as they had at the turn of the century, that immigrants would be willing to work for low wages, and would therefore take good jobs away from native-born Americans.

To address these fears, Congress passed the National Origins Act of 1924. This set limits and **quotas** that **discriminated** against particular ethnic groups, including Eastern Europeans and Asians. Behind the scenes, many pushed to keep out Jewish immigrants in particular. Such **anti-Semitism** was widespread, and some critics have suggested that Fitzgerald's unflattering portrayal of Wolfshiem, the novel's only major Jewish character, reflects these attitudes.

Some Americans felt threatened by the arrival of thousands of immigrants in the 1920s. Here, immigrants queue up at Ellis Island in New York.

African-American life

African-American characters have almost no presence in *The Great Gatsby*. This absence reflects the realities of racism in the 1920s.

Many African-Americans **migrated** north to escape the South, where **segregation** was still in place. The Ku Klux Klan was also strong in the South, hitting a peak number of four million members during the 1920s. The Klan is an extreme, pro-white organization with a history of violence toward blacks. Klansmen used to regularly perform lynchings, in which a group of people would torture and then kill an African American, usually by hanging.

In the North, where *The Great Gatsby* is set, the situation was better, but far from ideal. Most African Americans had to accept low-paying jobs and lived in the poorest areas. Prejudice was still common, and is shown in *The Great Gatsby* through Tom's fear of marriage between blacks and whites. Northern prejudice is perhaps also hinted at by Nick's reaction to the car full of African Americans, who try to compete with Gatsby's showy wealth.

THE HARLEM RENAISSANCE

In the 1920s, a group of African-American writers and artists began to focus on creating their own traditions, because they were excluded from many aspects of society at this time. In Harlem, in New York City, talented poets such as Claude McKay and Langston Hughes, authors such as Jean Toomer and Nella Larsen, and artists such as Aaron Douglas worked in a wide variety of styles. What united them was a desire to create art that expressed the realities of African-American life. This movement is remembered as "the Harlem Renaissance". Renaissance is Italian for rebirth.

The cover of *Opportunity* magazine, from June 1926, features art by Harlem Renaissance artist Aaron Douglas.

Class conflict

Fitzgerald's own life experiences – from Summit Avenue, to Princeton, to his girlfriends' parents – made him very aware of the elitism of US society. In fact, an examination of these elitist attitudes lies at the heart of *The Great Gatsby*.

"Old money" versus "new money"

The economic boom of the Roaring Twenties saw the creation of "new money", or people with recently made fortunes. In *The Great Gatsby*, Gatsby represents "new money", while Tom Buchanan represents "old money", or inherited family wealth. Geographically, the separateness of these two worlds is represented by West Egg and East Egg.

Tom is openly snobbish about Gatsby's gaudy displays of wealth, calling his yellow car a circus wagon and making fun of his pink suit. Tom makes clear that Gatsby, a "Mr. Nobody from Nowhere", cannot expect to gain access to the world of the Buchanans, no matter how wealthy he becomes.

The working classes often failed to benefit from the economic boom of the 1920s.

The working class

Even further from the Buchanans' world was the working class. During the 1920s, members of the working class were often overlooked in the rush to wealth. In rural areas, farmers were often out of work. More food was produced than was actually needed, and so many farmers found themselves left with crops that no one wanted to buy. Some of these workers migrated to cities to find work.

Often they could not find a place in this new world. In the novel, George Wilson, who is described as a ghost, embodies the rootless working class. Wilson lives in the valley of ashes, an undeveloped, depressing area where nothing grows or prospers. This represents a dumping ground for people who do not fit into an era made for the enjoyment of the elite.

HARDING AND COOLIDGE

Presidents Warren G. Harding (left, 1921–1923) and Calvin Coolidge (below, 1923–1929) did much to support the extremes of wealth and poverty seen in The Great Gatsby. Both men were enthusiastically pro-business. They helped pass laws that put fewer restrictions on big business, while siding against workers who were striking for better pay and working conditions. Taxes were lowered for the wealthy. Coolidge (twice) stopped laws that would have helped struggling farmers.

Different rules for different people

The true power of the upper class becomes clear at the end of the novel, when they destroy characters from outside their class. George Wilson's wife, Myrtle, is run over and killed by Daisy. Gatsby is shot dead by Wilson, because Tom directed him there. But, as Nick says, Tom and Daisy "smashed up things and creatures and then retreated back into their money or their vast carelessness". They leave town and face no punishment for their actions. Fitzgerald uses this story to suggest that US society in the 1920s was far from fair, or **egalitarian**. Instead, people like the Buchanans continued to live "safe and proud above the hot struggles of the poor".

For previous generations, life in the United States had been strongly rooted in community and religion. By the 1920s, however, society was becoming more urban and **secular**. Economic changes forced many people to move away from small-town, rural life. People instead moved to large cities, where they could find jobs in new industries, but where it was harder to find a close community. A guiding set of values, either moral or spiritual, was less certain than it had once been.

Materialism

At the core of *The Great Gatsby* is the idea that the Jazz Age generation threw away old-fashioned values, but failed to replace them with lasting values of its own. In particular, Fitzgerald explores the role of materialism in the Roaring Twenties. As the novel shows, material possessions began to give a kind of meaning to people's lives, filling the space left by traditional values.

In the 1920s, many people rushed to spend their money on the latest fashions.

The birth of advertising

The booming economy of the 1920s increased the spending habits of many Americans. As part of this, the era saw the birth of advertising.

In the 1920s, as more and more Americans had extra money to spend, companies began to make more of an effort to sell their products and to eliminate the competition. Advertising agencies developed slogans, billboards, and **celebrity endorsements**. They also got input from psychologists, who were aware that people linked products with feelings of fulfilment and self-worth.

Advertisements such as this reinforced a new desire for material goods in the 1920s.

Worshipping the dollar

In the novel, Myrtle connects material objects with identity and a sense of fulfilment. Her only pleasure seems to come from the possessions Tom buys for her, such as dresses and a furnished apartment, and she excitedly makes lists of all the things she needs to buy. Importantly, it is an expensive car that finally kills Myrtle. Through this symbol, Fitzgerald suggests that people like Myrtle could be ruined by their focus on material goods, a focus that replaced deeper, more lasting sources of happiness.

Gatsby's life also revolves around money and things. His mansion, cars, boats, and clothes are all status symbols that he hopes will make him seem like a member of the upper class, and therefore appeal to Daisy. Fitzgerald makes this clear in the scene in which Gatsby invites Daisy to see his mansion. In an exaggerated display of materialism, he starts throwing piles of his expensive shirts in the air.

Despite all his possessions, Gatsby lacks any true friends. At his funeral, only Nick, Gatsby's father, and a few others attend. Through this moment, Fitzgerald shows the emptiness of a life based strictly on material possessions.

The eyes of T. J. Eckleburg

Throughout the novel, the advertising hoarding featuring the gaze of the optician, T. J. Eckleburg, looms over the action, including the scene of Myrtle's death. After her death, George Wilson longs to find a greater sense of meaning in the world. Looking at the hoarding, he desperately insists that Eckleburg's eyes are the eyes of God, and that "God sees everything". His companion quickly points out that this is in fact just an advertisement, an example of a businessman trying to make more profit. This important scene highlights a central theme of the novel. In this immoral age, if people suddenly longed for old-fashioned moral or spiritual values, they found that such values had vanished, and were replaced by unfulfilling materialism.

Friedrich Nietzsche (1844–1900)

The German philosopher Friedrich Nietzsche (above) died in 1900, but his ideas would be felt throughout the 20th century. "God is dead" is perhaps his most famous statement. He meant that scientific advances had weakened society's roots in religion. Religion had once given meaning to people's lives. Now, without religion, Nietzsche believed that people were in danger of falling into **nihilism***, or the state of not having any particular values or a clear sense of right and wrong.*

In the world of The Great Gatsby, *it seems that Nietzsche's predictions have come true, as the Jazz Age culture is full of nihilists. The empty stare of T.J. Eckleburg symbolizes the absence of God watching over society, giving moral or spiritual direction.*

The American dream

Throughout US history, the "American dream" – the ability of any person to achieve success through hard work – has given purpose and meaning to many lives. For many critics, Gatsby represents this American dream, which could explain Fitzgerald's last-minute, patriotic choice of title, *Under the Red, White, and Blue*.

The idea of the "self-made man", or the person who achieves the American dream, has shaped US history and literature from its beginnings. In colonial America, Benjamin Franklin (1706–1790) embodied this ideal.

As he explained in his *Autobiography* (1791), Franklin was born into a poor family, yet he worked hard to improve himself, eventually becoming a successful politician, businessman, and inventor.

Fitzgerald connects Gatsby to Franklin through a list of self-improvement goals that Gatsby made as a boy. These goals parallel the "Thirteen Virtues" Franklin suggested in his *Autobiography*. For example, Franklin's "Cleanliness" equals Gatsby's "Bath every day", while his "Temperance" equals Gatsby's "No more [smoking] or chewing [tobacco]". Like Franklin, Gatsby believes that he can improve himself and create an identity he wants.

Fitzgerald included the ideas of Benjamin Franklin in *The Great Gatsby*. This helped connect Gatsby's story to the broader history of the United States.

The Emersonian self-made man

In the mid-19th century, Ralph Waldo Emerson (1803–1882) promoted Transcendentalism, a belief that there is a universal spirit, or god, all around us in nature. Emerson argued that, as we learn to recognize this spirit, we can also discover much about ourselves and our own sense of truth. In *Nature* (1836) he advised living by this personal sense of truth, saying, "Build, therefore, your own world. . . Conform your life to the pure idea in your mind." This advice again leads to a "self-made" person, recommending that people create their own ideal lives and futures.

Gatsby is a self-made man in that he lives by his own ideal truth – his dream to create a new, perfect future for himself and Daisy. Gatsby also builds his own world, complete with a new name and new fortune, in order to fully realize this dream. As Nick reflects, "So he invented just the sort of Jay Gatsby that a 17-year-old boy would be likely to invent, and to this conception [idea] he was faithful to the end."

Ralph Waldo Emerson was a Transcendentalist philospher and writer.

Killing the dream

On the surface, until the final scenes of the novel, Gatsby has achieved the American dream by becoming a self-made man. But, Fitzgerald seems to ask, what does this mean in an immoral age? For Franklin, personal success was supposed to benefit the larger community and make the nation great. In the novel's 1920s culture, however, "making it" has been tangled up with material possessions and parties. In Gatsby's case, it also means becoming involved in organized crime.

For Emerson, finding truth within oneself meant becoming connected to a greater sense of values that unites and improves people. Gatsby lives by his own truth, but his truth is shallow and self-centered: he focuses only on getting back a lost, youthful moment of happiness with Daisy, who is now married.

When Gatsby is murdered in his swimming pool, Fitzgerald perhaps suggests that the American dream itself is dead. The ideals of Franklin and Emerson have been replaced by materialism and a lack of core values. Nick captures this state of things in his final, dreamed image of West Egg: "Four solemn men in dress suits are walking along the sidewalk with a stretcher on which lies a drunken woman in a white evening dress. Her hand, which dangles over the side, sparkles cold with jewels. Gravely the men turn in at a house – the wrong house. But no one knows the woman's name, and no one cares."

In *The Great Gatsby*, Fitzgerald suggests that the western part of the USA had not been corrupted in the same way as the eastern states.

THE WEST

Throughout US history, frontiersmen kept exploring further west, searching for a new life. The West became a symbol of the American dream.

In The Great Gatsby, Fitzgerald often refers to the American West and the frontier. Dan Cody, the wealthy man who gave Gatsby his start, is described as a "pioneer" from the frontier. He may be named after Daniel Boone and William "Buffalo Bill" Cody, two legendary frontiersmen. Gatsby's boyhood notes for self-improvement were made on a copy of Hopalong Cassidy, a popular series of western cowboy stories. Nick calls himself "a pathfinder, an original settler". He returns to the West at the end of the novel, in hope of escaping the moral decay he saw in New York. Perhaps Fitzgerald hoped there were still traditional values in the West.

Modernism

After World War I, international artists of all kinds searched for new, truly modern ways to represent life – particularly urban life – in the 20th century. The term "modernism" has come to describe a movement, from about 1900 to 1945, when artists broke from tradition.

Fragmentation

A central feature of modernism was a sense of **fragmentation**. Artists felt that this reflected the lack of order and stability in modern life. Fragmentation can be seen in the cubist paintings of Pablo Picasso and Georges Braque, who broke their images apart into separate cubes. In literature, writers broke apart traditional techniques, such as a narrative that moves clearly from the first part of the story to the last. Some writers, such as Virginia Woolf and James Joyce, used a writing style called **stream of consciousness**, which seemed to be made up of random, rapid thoughts.

Cubist art such as *Portrait of Josette* by Juan Gris (1916) broke apart, or fragmented, the image.

While not as **experimental** as some modernists, Fitzgerald clearly used fragmentation in *The Great Gatsby*. Gatsby's story is told in bits and pieces that are not in order. The text begins with Nick talking about Gatsby after his death and then moves back and forth between past memories of Gatsby's early life and his later attempts to win back Daisy. On a deeper level, the novel is clearly about the fragmentation of traditional values.

Form

Imagery was also central to modernism. Artists such as Salvador Dalí created art full of strange, haunting images that recalled dreams. Inspired by writer Ezra Pound's instruction to "make it new", poets such as H. D. (Hilda Doolittle) tried to achieve a new kind of poetic imagery by describing objects in a cool, straightforward style that brought a clear picture to mind.

Throughout *The Great Gatsby*, Fitzgerald uses words in unexpected, poetic ways that capture a particular feeling or mood. For example, he describes "yellow cocktail music", "blue gardens", and how "a tray of cocktails floated at us through the twilight".

Fitzgerald's description of Daisy and Jordan in the Buchanans' breezy sitting room is especially famous. "The only completely stationary object in the room was an enormous couch on which two young women were buoyed up as though upon an anchored balloon. They were both in white, and their dresses were rippling and fluttering as if they had just been blown back in after a short flight around the house".

Symbolism was also central to modernist writers. In line with this, *The Great Gatsby* has many powerful, memorable symbols – such as the valley of ashes, clocks and time, flowers, and the eyes of T. J. Eckleburg. These give meaning and structure to the novel.

T.S. Eliot (1888–1965)

Fitzgerald considered the modernist T. S. Eliot (above) to be the "greatest of living poets". In his long poem "The Waste Land" (1922), Eliot conveyed the fragmented, meaningless nature of modern life. Fitzgerald's use of the depressed valley of ashes in The Great Gatsby *is believed to refer to Eliot's idea of modern life as a wasteland. Fitzgerald sent Eliot a copy of* The Great Gatsby, *and Eliot praised it highly.*

Life after *The Great Gatsby*

From 1925 to 1931, after the publication of *The Great Gatsby*, Fitzgerald continued to live mostly in Europe.

The Lost Generation

During this period, many **expatriate** US writers were living in Paris, including Ernest Hemingway and Gertrude Stein. In the period after *The Great Gatsby* was published, the Fitzgeralds informally became part of this circle in Paris. The writers in this group expressed disappointment with the direction the United States was taking – for many of the reasons explored in *The Great Gatsby*, such as its materialism and elitism. Most of these writers worked in the modernist style.

Ernest Hemingway (1899–1961)

*In 1924, Fitzgerald took an interest in helping along the career of a new young US writer named Ernest Hemingway (left). He did not meet Hemingway until the spring of 1925, when both men were living in Paris. The two writers could not be more different: Fitzgerald tried too hard to please and was a bit of a **dandy**, whereas Hemingway was known for his gruffness and rough masculinity. Nevertheless, the two spent a lot of time talking in Paris cafés, and Hemingway introduced Fitzgerald to the Stein circle.*

Over time, the status of the two men reversed. Hemingway became the most successful US novelist of his day, with books such as The Sun Also Rises *(1926) and* A Farewell to Arms *(1929), while Fitzgerald's fortunes took a turn for the worse. The two eventually became less close, but Fitzgerald later stated, "I always think of my friendship with [Hemingway] as being one of the high spots of my life". Hemingway would eventually become frustrated with Fitzgerald's sometimes wild behaviour, but he always admired his friend's*

Stein became a central figure for these expatriates, and her apartment became a meeting place where these writers exchanged ideas and attended all-night parties. She eventually invented the term "Lost Generation" to describe this group of Americans searching for meaning and a place to belong in the 1920s. Over the years, she consistently praised Fitzgerald's talent.

Burning out

Starting in 1926, Fitzgerald began writing his next novel, but he had trouble making progress. He and Zelda's constant parties had burned both of them out, and Fitzgerald had become an alcoholic. As in previous years, he had to focus on short stories to pay for their lavish lifestyle, and again his ambitions for another novel had to be put aside.

Zelda increasingly wanted to have her own identity, independent of her famous husband, and she took up painting, writing, and ballet as outlets for her creative expression. She began to focus obsessively on her ballet training, driving herself to exhaustion. She also began to display strange behaviour, such as talking about **hallucinations** as if they were real.

Critics rediscovered Zelda Fitzgerald's art, such as this self-portrait, which was probably first exhibited in 1942.

The crash

On 24 October, 1929, the US stock market crashed. Suddenly, many people found they could not pay their bank loans or afford their houses. In many ways, this was what Fitzgerald had predicted in *The Great Gatsby* – a nation that was so decadent was bound to fall apart. The period that followed this crash is known as the Great Depression, during which Americans struggled to find jobs and to provide for their families.

Depression

Although he had invested little in the stock market, Fitzgerald's personal life also took a downward turn during the Depression. In 1930, Zelda suffered a

nervous breakdown and had to be hospitalized. Doctors diagnosed her with the mental illness **schizophrenia**. She would spend the rest of her life in and out of mental hospitals. However, she did publish a largely autobiographical novel, *Save Me the Waltz*, in 1932, and continued to paint. Sadly, in March 1948, Zelda died while trapped during a fire at a mental hospital.

After the fun of the 1920s, life took a bad turn for Scott and Zelda in the 1930s.

Fitzgerald, meanwhile, was left to raise Scottie by himself and pay for Zelda's hospital treatment. After settling his family back in the United States in 1931, Fitzgerald lived on earnings from short stories as best he could, but he was often in debt. It was not until 1934, nine years after *The Great Gatsby*, that he published his next novel, *Tender Is the Night*. The book tells the somewhat autobiographical story of a married couple that suffers through too much drinking and the wife's mental illness. Many critics now consider this to be a great work, but it received mixed reviews at the time and did not sell very well.

The end

In 1936 Fitzgerald published a series of essays in *Esquire* magazine called "The Crack-up". In these painful, personal essays, he reflected on how he had risen so high, then fallen so far in his personal life and in the public eye.

These essays positioned Fitzgerald as a "has-been" in the publishing world, and so in 1937 he moved to Hollywood, where he hoped to work in films as a screenwriter. Throughout his career, Fitzgerald had made money by selling Hollywood the rights to his stories and novels, and so screenwriting seemed like a logical new career. However, his alcoholism sometimes got in the way of his work, and he achieved little success.

On 21 December, 1940, at the age of 44, Fitzgerald died of heart failure, a condition largely brought on by his drinking over the years. At the time, he was working on a novel, called *The Last Tycoon*, about a Hollywood movie executive.

When Fitzgerald died, apart from a few loyal friends in the publishing world, most people saw him as someone who had never lived up to his potential. Indeed, in many ways, his life was seen as a warning against living the lifestyle of the Jazz Age to its fullest.

As he got older, Fitzgerald struggled to retain his reputation as an important writer.

In a letter of June 12, 1940, to his daughter, Scottie, Fitzgerald reflected on how his career lost focus after *The Great Gatsby*, saying " I wish now I'd never relaxed or looked back, and said at the end of *The Great Gatsby*:

I've found my line—from now on this comes first. This is my immediate duty—without this I am nothing.

How *Gatsby* became great

During his own lifetime, Fitzgerald (below) achieved his greatest recognition with his first book, *This Side of Paradise*, but he was never able to recapture this level of success. After his death, people began to rediscover his writing, and his reputation began to be based on his third, relatively forgotten novel: *The Great Gatsby*.

First recognition

In 1941, Fitzgerald's college friend Edmund Wilson edited and published the unfinished *The Last Tycoon*, printing it in a volume that included *The Great Gatsby* and some of Fitzgerald's best short stories. Readers made a fresh discovery of Fitzgerald's talent. In 1942 the author James Thurber wrote, "Fitzgerald's perfection of style and form, as in *The Great Gatsby*, has a way of making something that lies between your stomach and your heart quiver a little". Over the course of the 1940s, several other editions of *The Great Gatsby* were published, and sales gradually improved. In 1949 a new film was made of the novel, starring the popular actor Alan Ladd.

LATER ADAPTATIONS

In 1974, another movie version of The Great Gatsby was released, this time featuring Robert Redford as Gatsby and Mia Farrow as Daisy (see page 49, opposite). While most critics felt it failed to capture the novel's intense emotions, the movie was very successful as a document of the look and feel of the period. Indeed, a generation of US moviegoers had their visual impression of the Roaring Twenties shaped by this movie.

Since then, operas, ballets, and television adaptations have been made, proving that The Great Gatsby by F. Scott Fitzgerald (left) continues to be a rich source of artistic inspiration.

The great American novel

The most important period of reassessment for Fitzgerald and *The Great Gatsby* came in the late 1940s and the 1950s. This period was similar to the 1920s, in that the United States emerged from a war (World War II, 1939–1945) in a position of economic and cultural power. The Roaring Twenties was, therefore, an age of great interest to this new generation, which was enjoying similar prosperity and new freedoms.

At the same time, American literary critics began work to establish a **canon** of great American literature. Up until this point, American literature was often seen as inferior to the work of European writers, but critics wanted to change this by studying and promoting works by native-born Americans. *The Great Gatsby* was well qualified to become of this newly formed canon of American literature, because of its focus on typically American themes of class, money, and big dreams, as well as Fitzgerald's beautiful writing style. In 1950 the important US literary critic Lionel Trilling wrote, "*The Great Gatsby* . . . after a quarter-century is still as fresh as when it first appeared; it has even gained in weight and relevance, which can be said of few American books of its time."

By the 1960s, *The Great Gatsby* had become a standard book for US school and university students, and many people claimed that it was one of the greatest American novels of all time. Overseas, audiences also began to read and appreciate it. Critics continued to examine the novel over the next decades, often looking at it in new ways or relating it to current issues, such as **feminism**.

A lasting achievement

Today, there are more copies of *The Great Gatsby* sold each year than were sold in Fitzgerald's lifetime. This masterpiece of American literature has at last allowed Fitzgerald to achieve his own definition of greatness: "The wise writer writes for the youth of his own generation, the critics of the next, and the schoolmasters of ever afterward."

The 1974 film of *The Great Gatsby*, starring Mia Farrow and Robert Redford, inspired a new generation to think about the 1920s.

TIMELINE

1896	Francis Scott Key Fitzgerald is born in St. Paul, Minnesota, on 24 September.
1900	Zelda Sayre is born in Montgomery, Alabama, 24 July.
1908	Fitzgerald enters the St. Paul Academy in September.
1911	Fitzgerald enters the Newman School in Hackensack, New Jersey.
1913	Fitzgerald enters Princeton University in Princeton, New Jersey.
1914	World War I begins in August.
1915	Fitzgerald meets Ginevra King in St. Paul in January.
1917	Fitzgerald joins the US Army in October.
1918	Fitzgerald reports for training camp at Camp Sheridan, near Montgomery, Alabama, in June. Fitzgerald meets Zelda Sayre in July.
1918	World War I ends on 11 November.
1919	Congress approves the 18th Amendment, "Prohibition", banning alcohol in the United States.
1920	Zelda Sayre and Fitzgerald are married in New York City on 3 April. Fitzgerald's *Flappers and Philosophers*, a collection of short stories, is published in September.
1920	The 19th Amendment of 26 August gives women the right to vote.
1921	Fitzgerald's daughter, Scottie, is born on 26 October.
1922	Fitzgerald's *The Beautiful and Damned* is published on 4 March. Fitzgerald's *Tales of the Jazz Age*, a collection of short stories, is published in September.
1922	Fitzgerald moves in October to Great Neck, New York, where he starts works on *The Great Gatsby*.
1923	Fitzgerald's play, *The Vegetable*, premieres (and fails).
1924	Fitzgerald and his family leave for Europe in the spring. During this period, he finishes *The Great Gatsby*. Fitzgerald's "Absolution", a short story containing text cut from *The Great Gatsby*, is published in June.
1925	Fitzgerald's *The Great Gatsby* is published on 10 April. The initial reviews are mixed.
1925	Fitzgerald first meets Ernest Hemingway in Paris in May. The Fitzgeralds become part of the group of expatriate writers, called the Lost Generation, that surrounds writer Gertrude Stein.

1926	A film adaptation of *The Great Gatsby* premieres.
1926	Fitzgerald's *All the Sad Young Men*, a collection of short stories, is published in February.
1926	A theatre adaptation of *The Great Gatsby* premieres in February.
1929	The stock market crashes on 24 October. The Great Depression follows.
1930	Zelda Fitzgerald has a nervous breakdown in April and begins treatment. She will have major breakdowns again in 1932 and 1934 and spend much of the rest of her life in mental hospitals.
1931	After years back and forth between Europe and the United States, the Fitzgeralds return to the United States in September.
1932	Fitzgerald settles near Baltimore, Maryland, in May while Zelda lives in various treatment centres.
1934	Fitzgerald's *Tender Is the Night* is published on 12 April.
1935	Fitzgerald's *Taps at Reveille*, a collection of short stories, is published in March.
1936	Fitzgerald publishes his "Crack-up" essays in *Esquire* magazine.
1937	Fitzgerald moves to Hollywood in July to work as a screenwriter.
1940	Fitzgerald dies of heart failure, aged 44, on 21 December.
1940s	Several new editions of *The Great Gatsby* are published.
1941	*The Last Tycoon*, Fitzgerald's unfinished novel, is published on October 27 in a volume that includes *The Great Gatsby* and several short stories.
1948	Zelda Fitzgerald dies in a hospital fire on 10 March.
1949	A film adaptation of *The Great Gatsby* premieres, starring Alan Ladd.
Late 1940s and 1950s	Critics begin to discover *The Great Gatsby*, with many deciding it is one of American literature's most important works.
1960s	*The Great Gatsby* becomes widely read in US schools and universities. It also gains international recognition.
1974	A film adaptation of *The Great Gatsby* featuring Robert Redford premieres.
1986	Scottie Fitzgerald Lanahan Smith, Fitzgerald's only child, dies on 18 June.
1996	The centennial (100th anniversary) of Fitzgerald's birth is marked by celebrations and new critical examinations.

FURTHER INFORMATION

The edition used in the writing of this book is *The Great Gatsby* (Scribners, 1995).

Other works by F. Scott Fitzgerald

Novels
This Side of Paradise [first published 1920]. (Signet Classics, 2006)
The Beautiful and Damned [first published 1922]. (Penguin Books, 2004)
Tender is the Night: A Romance [first published 1934]. (Penguin Books, 2005)
The Last Tycoon (Unfinished) [first published 1941]. (Penguin Books, 2004)

Short story collections
The Cambridge Edition of the Works of F. Scott Fitzgerald. (Cambridge University Press, 2000). This contains many of Fitzgerald's short stories, including:
Flappers and Philosophers
Tales of the Jazz Age
All the Sad Young Men

Plays
The Vegetable. (Macmillan USA ,1987)

Books about Fitzgerald, *The Great Gatsby*, and the 1920s

Barks, Cathy W. *Dear Scott, Dearest Zelda: The Love Letters of F. Scott and Zelda Fitzgerald* (Bloomsbury, 2003)
Blackman, Cally. *The Twenties and Thirties: Flappers and Vamps* (Heinemann Library, 2000)
Curnutt, Kirk. *Historical Guide to F. Scott Fitzgerald* (Oxford University Press, USA, 2004)
Handyside, Christopher. *A History of Jazz, A History of American Music* (Heinemann Library, 2006)
Hixson, Walter L. *Charles A. Lindbergh: Lone Eagle* (Longman, 2003)
Levy, Patricia, Sheehan, Sean. *From Speakeasies to Stalinism (the early 1920s to mid-1930s.* (Modern Eras Uncovered) (Raintree, 2005)
Prigozy, Ruth. *F. Scott Fitzgerald* (Gerald Duckworth & Co Ltd, 2004)

Fitzgerald websites

www.sc.edu/fitzgerald
The University of Carolina's site has lots of information on F. Scott Fitzgerald's life and works, from film clips to quotations.
www.online-literature.com/fitzgerald
Under "Fiction", click on "The Great Gatsby" for a useful summary of the novel.
www.fitzgeraldsociety.org
The International F. Scott Fitzgerald Society website has details about Scott and Zelda's lives.

Places to contact

F. Scott and Zelda Fitzgerald Museum
919 Felder Ave
Montgomery, Alabama 36106
Set in a house where the Fitzgeralds briefly lived in the early 1930s, this museum contains photographs, letters, and paintings by Zelda.

Documentaries

F. Scott Fitzgerald: The American Dreamer (2004)
F. Scott Fitzgerald: Winter Dreams (2002)

Films

The Great Gatsby (1974)
Directed by Jack Clayton, starring major actors Robert Redford and Mia Farrow.

abstract made to look less realistic and more expressive or decorative

alliance agreement to be on the same side of a conflict

Anglo-Saxon person descended from the Anglo-Saxons, Germanic peoples who invaded and settled in England in the 5th century AD

anti-Semitism prejudice against Jewish people

assembly line method of production in which a product is made by a line of workers and machines that each have specific tasks

autobiographical work that tells a person's own life story

aviation use of airplanes

blues style of music originating in the early 20th century. It is characterized by a slow rhythm and often sad lyrics.

bob short haircut for women, usually cut to just below the ears

bond in finance, a contract issued by government agencies or private companies saying that a person has loaned them money and will receive it back with interest (extra money)

bootlegger person who makes and sells alcohol illegally, often for profit

canon group of important works of literature

celebrity endorsements when a famous person agrees to be in an advertisement for a product

colonial period in American history before Independence in 1776

conform make something fit a certain expectation

corrupt immoral

corset tight-fitting underwear worn by women to create a slender figure

critic person who writes about and analyses literature

dandy man who loves looking good

decadent focused on pleasure, often in the sense of spending a lot of money to achieve it

definitive best or most detailed source on something

discriminate treat someone differently based on factors such as race or religion

disillusioned made to lose faith or lose trust in something

editor person who reads an author's writing and makes suggestions to improve it

egalitarian belief that everyone is equal and should have the same opportunities

elite best or most privileged

elitism snobbery, or the belief that only the most privileged should have access to certain opportunities

embody represent

expatriate person living in a country that is not his or her native country

experimental breaking away from traditional styles and trying new things

fast living in a careless way, focusing on fun

feminism movement that works to improve the role and rights of women in society

flapper young woman in the 1920s who wore the latest fashions and enjoyed a carefree lifestyle

flashback device by which an author suddenly moves the story back to an earlier moment in time

fragmentation breaking apart into pieces

gaudy flashy or showy

hallucination dream or fantasy that seems real

heir person who stands to inherit something, such as the title of king

heroine female hero or main character

imagery images created by an author or artist to represent certain things

immigrant person who settles in a new country

immigration process of moving to and settling in a new country

improvise perform without a set plan or script

intricate complicated, with many parts involved

jazz style of music that originated with African Americans in the first decades of the 20th century. Over time, it has taken on many forms, but it was originally characterized by lively rhythms and improvisation

lavish very expensive or luxurious

material possessions items that a person can buy and own

materialism focus on acquiring material possessions, especially valuing these possessions above everything else

migrate move somewhere else, perhaps in search of work

modernism style of art and literature in the first half of the 20th century characterized by personal expression and breaking from old styles

narrator character who tells the story

neutral not taking sides or getting involved in a conflict

nihilism philosophy of not having any particular values or a sense of right and wrong

organized crime network of people who work together to commit crimes

phonograph an early type of record player that reproduced sound by running a needle over a grooved disk

Prohibition name for the 18th Amendment to the US Constitution, which passed in 1919 and banned the making or sale of alcohol in the United States

prosperity having a lot of money

quest goal that is pursued

quota set limit on something – for example, the number of people allowed into a country

ragtime style of music originating with African Americans that was popular in the first two decades of the 20th century. It was characterized by extremely lively piano compositions.

rig illegally make an event, such as a sporting match, have a certain result

schizophrenia mental illness characterized by hallucinations and a separation from reality

secular not focused on religion

segregation system in which people of different races are kept separate in most aspects of life

sentimental overly emotional

Serb native of Serbia, a country that was a neighbor to the Austro-Hungarian Empire before World War I

Slav member of the Slavic-speaking peoples of eastern and southeastern Europe

stock market crash the stock market is an organized system through which people sell shares of ownership in US and foreign companies. When the market crashed in 1929, the value of these shares fell dramatically, leaving people who had bought them with little or nothing.

stream of consciousness style of writing that sounds like random, rapid thoughts

stylized made to look dramatic or interesting, rather than natural

suitor admirer

superficial based on surface appearances only and not on deeper values

supremacy being the most powerful

symmetry having forms arranged in a balanced, regular way

tabloid small newspaper with lots of photographs that contains brief articles, and often focuses on scandal and gossip

Victorian period of history when Queen Victoria ruled the British Empire (1837–1901). The term also implies the conservative values of this period.

youth culture activities, fashions, music, and trends favoured by young people

INDEX

Titles in the *History in Literature* series include:

CHARLES DICKENS'
OLIVER TWIST

Hardback   0 431 08137 3

F. SCOTT FITZGERALD'S
THE GREAT GATSBY

Hardback   0 431 08170 0

ANNE HOLM'S
I AM DAVID

Hardback   0 431 08169 7

HARPER LEE'S
TO KILL A MOCKINGBIRD

Hardback   0 431 08173 5

GEORGE ORWELL'S
ANIMAL FARM

Hardback   0 431 08168 9

ERICH MARIA REMARQUE'S
**ALL QUIET ON THE
WESTERN FRONT**

Hardback   0 431 08175 1

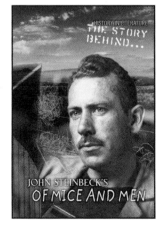

JOHN STEINBECK'S
OF MICE AND MEN

Hardback   0 431 08172 7

MARK TWAIN'S
**ADVENTURES
OF HUCKLEBERRY FINN**

Hardback   0 431 08171 9

Find out about other titles from Heinemann Library on our website www.heinemann.co.uk/library